FAVORITE HORSE BREEDS

CLYDESDALE HORSES

by Cari Meister

AMICUS | AMICUS INK

Amicus High Interest and Amicus Ink are published by Amicus
P.O. Box 1329, Mankato, MN 56002
www.amicuspublishing.us

Library of Congress Cataloging-in-Publication Data
Names: Meister, Cari, author.
Title: Clydesdale horses / by Cari Meister.
Description: Mankato, Minnesota : Amicus, [2019] | Series: Favorite horse
  breeds | Audience: K to grade 3. | Includes index.
Identifiers: LCCN 2017027595 (print) | LCCN 2017031604 (ebook) | ISBN
  9781681515076 (pdf) | ISBN 9781681514253 (library binding) | ISBN
  9781681523453 (paperback) | ISBN 9781681515076 (ebook)
Subjects: LCSH: Clydesdale horse--Juvenile literature.
Classification: LCC SF293.C65 (ebook) | LCC SF293.C65 M45 2019 (print) |
  DDC 636.1/5--dc23
LC record available at https://lccn.loc.gov/2017027595

Photo Credits: Juniors/Superstock cover; Melory S/123RF 2; Colin
Monteath/Minden 5; Brad Hargreaves/Shutterstock 6; Travel Ink/Getty
8–9; Mary Evans/Grenville Collins Postcard Collection/MaryEvans 10–11;
Ory Photography/Shutterstock 13; Tamara Gooch/Alamy 14; Joy Brown/
Shutterstock 17; Mark Langford/Getty 18–19; Paul Keleher from Mass,
US/CommonsWikipedia 21; C.Slawik/Juniors/Alamy 22

Editor: Wendy Dieker
Designer: Veronica Scott
Photo Researcher: Holly Young

Printed in China

HC 10 9 8 7 6 5 4 3 2 1
PB 10 9 8 7 6 5 4 3 2 1

TABLE OF CONTENTS

A Tall Horse   4

Big Feet   7

Draft Horses   8

Pulling Power   11

Winter Ready   12

Feathers   15

A Big Eater   16

Big Babies   19

In the Parade   20

How Do You Know
  it's a Clydesdale Horse?   22

Words to Know   23

Learn More   24

Index   24

A TALL HORSE

It is hard to miss a Clydesdale. It is very big! It can be up to 18 hands tall. That is about 6 feet (1.8 m) from the ground to its **withers**.

Did You Know?

A horse has a bony bump where the mane meets its back. This is called the withers.

BIG FEET

A Clydesdale has very big feet. Its **horseshoes** are the size of dinner plates! One shoe can weigh 5 pounds (2.3 kg). It is twice the size of a racehorse shoe.

DRAFT HORSES

Clydesdales are from Scotland. It is a heavy **draft horse**. It worked on farms. It pulled plows. It is a powerful horse.

PULLING POWER

In cities, teams of Clydesdales pulled wagons. Soldiers used them in war. These horses could pull cannons. They pulled heavy carts of gear.

WINTER READY

Clydesdales were made for
winter. They have a thick coat.
It helps keep the horse warm.
They have thick manes and
tails, too.

FEATHERS

Clydesdales have long hair on their lower legs. It is often white. It can be brown. It can be black. It helps keep their legs warm.

Did You Know?

The long hair on a Clydesdale's legs is called "feathers."

A BIG EATER

A Clydesdale needs to eat a lot. It eats grass in the **pasture**. It also eats grain and **hay**. Clydesdales eat 20 to 50 pounds (9 to 23 kg) of hay a day!

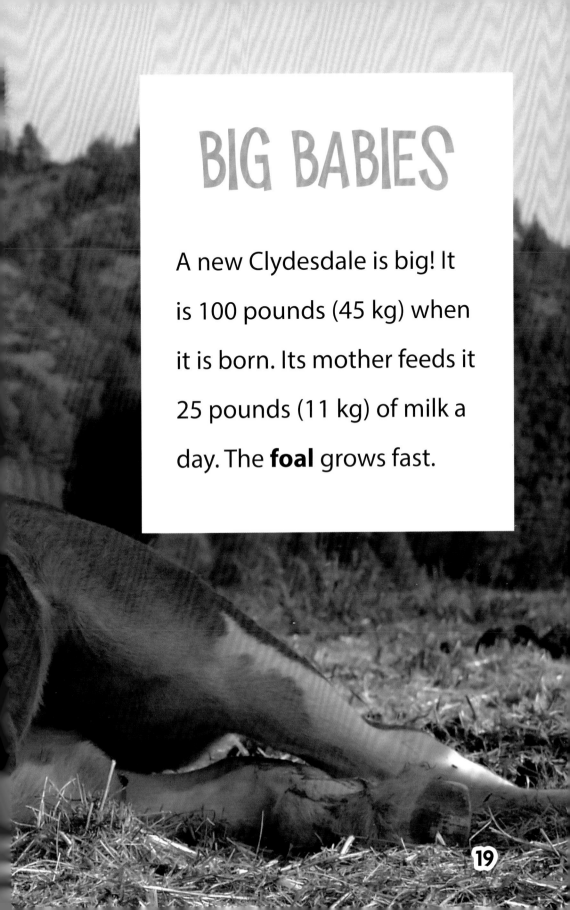

BIG BABIES

A new Clydesdale is big! It is 100 pounds (45 kg) when it is born. Its mother feeds it 25 pounds (11 kg) of milk a day. The **foal** grows fast.

IN THE PARADE

Clydesdales are big and strong. But they are graceful and fun to ride. You might see these gentle giants all dressed up at a parade!

HOW DO YOU KNOW IT'S A CLYDESDALE HORSE?

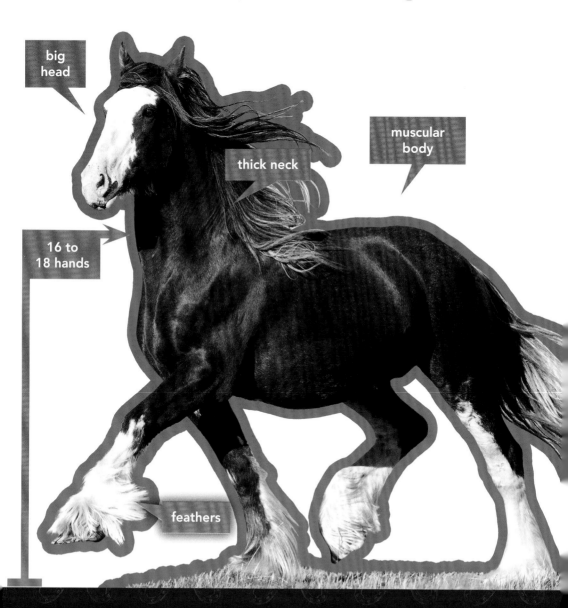

big head

muscular body

thick neck

16 to 18 hands

feathers

WORDS TO KNOW

draft horse – a tall, powerful horse that is bred to pull carts and equipment.

foal – baby horse.

hay – dried grass that farmers and ranchers feed their animals.

horseshoe – a curved piece of metal nailed to a horse's hoof to help protect the hoof and give grip.

pasture – an open grassy area where farm and ranch animals can run and eat grass.

withers – the bony part where the base of the horse's mane meets its back.

LEARN MORE

Books

Dell, Pamela. *Clydesdales*. North Mankato, Minn.: Child's World, 2014.

Hansen, Grace. *Clydesdale Horses*. Minneapolis: Abdo Kids, 2016.

Kolpin, Molly. *Favorite Horses: Breeds Girls Love*. North Mankato, Minn.: Capstone, 2015.

Websites

A Clydesdale Horse Profile
https://www.thespruce.com/meet-the-clydesdale-1886108

Girl's Horse Club
http://www.girlshorseclub.com/

INDEX

coat 12

eating 16

feathers 15
foals 19

hair 12, 15
history 8, 11
horseshoes 7

parades 20
pulling 8, 11

size 4, 7, 22

withers 4